Desirée Mays
Opera Unveiled
2003

♪

ART FORMS INC.
Santa Fe · Salt Lake City

Art Forms Inc.
Opera Unveiled 2003 © by Art Forms Inc.
Text copyright © Desirée Mays

Cover design and layout by Pieter Hull
Rear cover photograph by Carolyn Wright

First edition

ISBN 0-9707822-2-5

To order copies of *Opera Unveiled 1999 - 2003*
please send a check for $15 (postage included) to:
Art Forms, Inc., 31 Valencia Loop
Santa Fe, New Mexico 87508
Fax: (505) 466 1908
Email: dmays@attglobal.net

Contents

to
my mother, *Sheila*,
and my sisters,
Vanessa and *Diana*,
with love

♪

La Belle Hélène

Jacques Offenbach

Beauty is nothing without a little abandon.
                                    – La Belle Hélène

L'amour, la belle France, and *l'opéra bouffe* pretty much sum up the exciting, naughty world inhabited and perhaps exploited by Jacques Offenbach. How Jakob, son of the former Isaac Juda Eberst, a cantor and musician of Cologne, became the personification of French operetta in the second half of the 19th century is one of opera's great stories. It tells of determination, guts, belief in oneself and in a dream – a story of extreme poverty that transformed itself into enormous success, then dove into failure, and leveled out only shortly before the composer's death. Offenbach was a man whose joyous music enchanted Paris at a wildly frivolous period of French history; who, night

"There gapes a little cavernous opening which by night is lighted by superior gas and the brilliant promise of good cheer. It is the David of opera houses which scatters more wounds amongst its big rivals than they would care to acknowledge. You laugh when you get inside the theatre at its tiny proportions. A gentleman in the orchestra stalls might converse in a whisper with his friends in the gallery. But people come for the brightest and newest music that the French stage affords. And they are never disappointed. Absolutely never."

Opéra bouffe, for which Offenbach became so famous, took its very name from Offenbach's Théâtre Bouffes-Parisiens, and was developed solely by him in reaction to the more formalized *opéra-comique*. Opéra bouffe is comic opera in which witty and sophisticated spoken dialogue is combined with light, sparkling music. The golden age of both opéra bouffe and operetta (*opérette* in French), with their romantic tales and happy endings, saw its heyday in the latter years of the 19th century, and came to an abrupt end in the upheaval of World War I. Following the war, musical comedies, both British and American, made their debut as the next step in the evolution of light opera.

Offenbach was fortunate to team up with Ludovic Halévy and Henri Meilhac, outstanding librettists who wrote witty and sophisticated books satirizing the Paris of Napoleon III. (Years later, Halévy and Meilhac wrote the libretto for Bizet's *Carmen*.) In addition to finding the best librettists, Offenbach had a gift for spotting new, young, gifted singers. His discovery of the beautiful and talented singer-comédienne Hortense Schneider completed the team which was to work together for many years on many productions.

Schneider made a nervous debut at the Bouffes-Parisiens at age 22, a month after the theatre opened, and audiences and critics raved about her from the start. Thanks to Offenbach, she became the reigning sex symbol of Paris overnight, and threw herself with equal abandon into the life of the theatre and numerous love affairs. Her list of noble, wealthy lovers grew quickly, causing a malicious rival to name her "Passage des Princes." Even the influential Duc de Morny loved her, in a relationship that lasted for years.

Offenbach's irresistibly catchy melodies were whistled and sung in the streets of Paris. He laced his popular music with the saucy satire that became his trademark. Never vicious, his satire, spicy and lighthearted, was always presented in a spirit of fun. Contemporary composers, Wagner, Meyerbeer, the court, the establishment – all came under his satirical eye, and all laughed with Offenbach. Paris was happy to laugh at herself in those days, and Offenbach provided the means.

Soon, the Bouffes-Parisiens was too small. Offenbach opened another, larger theatre nearby, and transformed it, too, into a place of glamour. But there were limitations. His license, as a producer of *opérette*, specified that he could present only one-act pieces with no more than four player-singers. When, in 1858, the censor lifted these restrictions, Offenbach composed his first two-act operetta, *Orphée aux Enfers* (Orpheus in the Underworld). The orchestra was increased to 30 musicians, and the productions included 20 to 30 musical numbers. Offenbach produced operettas on a grand scale, sparing no expense on either his theatres or his productions. As a result, he often found himself on the verge of bankruptcy.

The phenomenal success of *Orphée* launched Offenbach on the path to lasting fame. In it, he parodied not only gods and goddesses but the entire French social system. In Offenbach's version of the mythic tale, Eurydice is a flirt bored to tears by her husband's eternal playing of "celestial" music on his violin. She is carried off to Hades by Pluto, lord of the underworld, with whom she has a passionate affair. Orphée is delighted to be free of his flirtatious wife, but Public Opinion insists, for the sake of decency, that he must retrieve her. As the gods party in Hades to the tune of graceful minuets transformed into wild can-cans, Orphée arrives – but Eurydice doesn't want to leave with him. The gods (other than Pluto, that is) insist that the mortal woman follow her husband back to earth. As the couple is about to leave Hades, Pluto hurls a thunderbolt that strikes the ground behind Orphée's heels, causing him to look around and so lose his wife forever, in accordance with the ancient myth.

Musicians complained bitterly of the "insult" to Greek myth and to Gluck's immortal opera, *Orfeo ed Euridice*. People were "shocked" at the licentious behavior of the gods and goddesses – and everyone rushed to see Offenbach's latest outrageous offering. With a deep understanding of the interests of his audience, this astute composer gave them what they wanted: laughter edged with naughtiness, and pure enjoyment. Rossini saw *Orphée* and was so impressed that he dubbed Offenbach the "Mozart of the Boulevards."

Offenbach's modus operandi was to compose day and night, often in the company of other people and usually surrounded by his growing family. He averaged five operettas a year between 1855 and 1875, most of them successful productions. His bright wit and sense of play never faltered. Yet Offenbach understood the fickleness of his audiences and the ephemeral nature of his compositions. He said, "The operetta that's brought to life throws into oblivion the one that precedes it. It's like a series of pictures that dissolve, as in a magic lantern, and once past, the greatest success weighs no more heavily on the spectator's mind than the most sensational failure." *La Belle Hélène* made its appearance in the midst of all this creativity in 1864, to be followed by *La Vie Parisienne* in 1866, and *La Grande-Duchesse de Gérolstein*, a satire on the military, in 1867.

La Belle Hélène was Offenbach's second foray into the world of Greek myth. The team of Offenbach, Henri Meilhac (who structured the main frame of the plots), and Ludovic Halévy (who wrote the verses for the musical numbers) chose Helen of Troy as a ripe subject for Offenbach's special treatment. Helen, the daughter of Leda and Zeus (who was disguised as a swan in that particular liaison), was married to the rather stolid Menelaus, King of Sparta. She fell in love with Paris as a result of the divine intervention of Venus, who had promised to give Paris (son of Priam, King of Troy) the most beautiful woman in the world after Paris chose Venus as the most beautiful of three goddesses. Paris arrived at the court of Menelaus and carried Helen off to Troy, thus sparking the Trojan War. That's the Greek version of the myth.

In Offenbach's version, *La Belle Hélène* opens with lively can-can music that fades into a lovely waltz, bright and inviting, only to be enfolded once again into the can-can. The scene is ancient Greece with temples, fires on tripods, Greeks bearing gifts. "Towards thy altars, Jupie, we hasten," calls the disrespectful chorus. Calchas, the high priest, complains that there are too many flowers. "What have sacrifices come to? They used to bring us oxen and sheep!" The gorgeous Hélène appears, leading mourners in a ritual sacrifice in honor of the death of Adonis. "Venus, hear us, we must have love even though it no longer lives in the world," Hélène cries, launching into her first aria. This is all tongue-in-cheek, of course, for when Calchas approaches, Hélène halts the sacrifice: "It can wait." She is far more interested in learning from Calchas what happened on Mount Ida, for she has heard that Venus promised there to give Paris the most beautiful woman in the world, and is not Hélène that woman? "Is the story true?" she asks Calchas. "That seems to be the case," he replies.

(This section is spoken dialogue, conducted in conversational tones, as is usual in operetta: a series of musical numbers interspersed with spoken dialogue. In order for English-speaking audiences to understand the dialogue, many opera companies today, including The Santa Fe Opera, present the musical numbers in the original French, the dialogue in English. This is not as odd as it may sound. For comic dialogue to work, the audience must be able to understand the words.)

Hélène is delighted by this exciting turn of events. Knowing she will be called a coquette no matter what she does, she shrugs her shoulders saying, "It is the will of Fate! The daughter of a bird, how could I be anything else but a flirt?" Orestes, son of Agamemnon, who is sung by a mezzo-soprano, enters, bent on chasing the vestal virgins. Calchas holds him at bay.

Moments later, Calchas is interrupted by a shepherd, who asks if he has received a letter from Venus. (The gods write letters?) "No," says Calchas. "That's odd, the dove left before me," says the shepherd, who is actually Paris in disguise. The dove flies in on cue and alights on Paris's hand, a letter in its beak. The letter is from Venus, and in it the goddess instructs Calchas to introduce Paris to Hélène.

Paris recounts how he offered Venus an apple as the sign of his choice of her over the other goddesses. His aria, in strict waltz rhythm, "Au mont Ida," is one of the opera's many highlights. Hélène appears and asks Calchas about the handsome shepherd she has seen him talking to. When Calchas hesitates, Hélène speaks directly to the shepherd: "How do you come to be here?" He tells her he entered a contest in the hopes of being noticed. "For your beauty?" Hélène asks. "No, for my intelligence," Paris replies, usually to laughter from the audience. As Hélène and Paris look deeply into one another's eyes they are interrupted by the March of the Kings and the royal entrances of Kings Ajax I and II, Achilles ("I'd feel much more at ease if it weren't for my sore heel!"), Agamemnon, and Hélène's husband, Menelaus.

The Kings of Greece arrive not to a noble air, but to music in which marked strains of the can-can can be heard. The Kings have gathered to play a game, the purpose of which is to discover an intelligent man. An out-of-tune fanfare announces the start of the competition. In a parody of competitions portrayed in grand opera (*Tannhäuser* in particular), Menelaus announces four clues: "What is it cows do? What is the abbreviation of *county*? What surrounds a castle that is sometimes filled with water, and what is another name for a quarrel or a small outburst?" The kings, like children, argue over the clues. Then Paris, the shepherd, steps forward with the answer: "Locomotive" (*Low-co-moat-tiff*).

The kings wonder about the shepherd's identity. Referring to the contest of the beautiful goddesses, Paris tells them he is the man with the apple, the son of King Priam. This sets the entire cast off into a hilarious finale, led by Hélène, on the theme of "L'homme à la pomme" (the man with the apple – it doesn't rhyme so well in English). Hélène joyfully crowns Paris the winner of the contest and invites him to dinner. A clap of thunder is heard and Calchas, the oracle, who is in league with Paris, announces that Menelaus must leave and go for a month to Crete. As everyone sends the puzzled Menelaus off to Crete, his wife, Hélène, bids him farewell: "Be off, ducky, anywhere." Menelaus and Hélène kiss goodbye with the expectant Paris looking on as the curtain falls.

Act II opens with Hélène dressing in a high-necked gown to "immure her grace and beauty." Hélène wonders, in a token effort to protect her marriage, "Why, O Venus, have you chosen our ill-fated family to carry out your experiments?" She ends her glorious Invocation to Venus by asking her servant to show Paris into her presence. When Paris sees the high-necked dress, he is skeptical, and wonders aloud whether Hélène truly is the most beautiful woman in the world. The ploy works; the insulted Hélène will now go to any lengths to prove that, indeed, she is.

Paris leaves as the Kings are again announced. This time, they have assembled to play the Game of the Goose. They take their places and Calchas is soon caught cheating for playing with loaded dice – the high priest! The game ends in chaos, and Hélène, left alone with Calchas, suggests that she might now sleep. She tells him that what she really wants is to dream of Paris, whom she adores. Calchas gets the message. Hélène lies down to sleep, and as Paris appears, dressed as a slave, Calchas turns a blind eye and leaves. Paris plays Hélène's game of the dream in a melting duet, even when the "dreaming" Hélène cross-examines him on the subject of Venus. In what ways is the goddess more beautiful? Paris lists the ways, ending with the news that it was Venus's kiss that made him choose her as the most beautiful goddess. Hélène throws herself into Paris's arms – just as Menelaus appears in the doorway, newly returned from Crete.

Hélène's dream is shattered, and Menelaus is flabbergasted and furious. He calls the Kings, who come bumbling in, all of them more than a little merry from copious Greek libations, and with crowns of roses on their heads. A long discussion ensues regarding Menelaus's honor parodying a perennial theme in Greek mythology. Finally, at Hélène's prompting, the Kings decide that it is all Menelaus's fault for coming home so unexpectedly. In what sounds like pure Gilbert and Sullivan (whose first operetta, *Thespis*, premiered in 1871, only seven years after *La Belle Hélène*), Hélène lectures her husband, telling him that he should have given prior warning of his return. That way, "A man of honor avoids all this unpleasantness." The Kings then turn on Paris and order him to leave – "A vile seducer insults and outrages us," sing the Kings to a wildly infectious waltz as, in the best tradition of Rossinian crescendo, the act ends.

Act III is set by the seaside, where the people of Greece are drinking, singing, and being generally outrageous. Orestes reports that, because Venus is angry with Menelaus for sending Paris away, she has imposed a huge bacchanal on Greece. "Venus has released subtle emanations which make husbands leave their wives and wives their husbands. All is pleasure and debauchery." Menelaus, however, is interested only in his own wife's behavior. He demands an explanation, but Hélène stalls. "Stop fussing about a dream," she tells him. "If you don't, I'll cause you to make a fuss about the real thing." Menelaus stands his ground. In a patriotic trio that is a parody of the great trio in Rossini's *Guillaume Tell*, Agamemnon and Calchas insist that an end be put to the debauchery. "It can't last much longer," they insist – prophetic words for both Offenbach and the Second Empire.

The Kings propose that Menelaus sacrifice himself for the greater good. "Humankind must be served!" they insist. But Menelaus, who is not about to sacrifice himself for anyone, has a plan. He tells his friends that the High Priest of Venus is on his way to sort things out. The chorus announces the approach of the High Priest, who turns out to be Paris in yet another disguise. He enters, yodeling, and predicts that all will return to normal if Queen Hélène will take a little journey to the island of Cythera, where she must sacrifice white heifers to Venus. Menelaus, delighted with this simple solution, agrees at once without consulting his wife. When Hélène appears, she is not inclined to go quietly. "Why should I go when it is you, not I, who has angered Venus?" This sets off a hilarious bit of stage business during which the High Priest/Paris lets her know who he is. As soon as she catches on, Hélène agrees to leave at once. She boards the ship with Paris, who, once the ship clears the dock, throws off his disguise and announces, "I am Paris. Wait for her no more, Menelaus, I am taking her away." And thus, as the opera ends, the Trojan War begins.

Offenbach was determined that only one woman could play Hélène, and that woman was Hortense Schneider. But Schneider, now a big star, had just decided to leave Paris and return to Bordeaux. Offenbach pleaded with her, playing Hélène's arias until she could resist no longer. "I'll play Hélène," she later wired him, "for 2000 francs a month" – in those days, an exorbitant fee. Offenbach agreed. "Come immediately," he wired back.

During rehearsals for that first production of *La Belle Hélène*, Schneider pulled every trick in the prima donna's handbook. Impossible to work with, she started up a personal vendetta with Lea Silly, the mezzo-soprano who sang Orestes; the two women fought and upstaged each other at every opportunity. Offenbach, who personally directed the production, ignored the battle. He had seen it all before, and was rewarded for his perseverance on opening night,

December 17, 1864, when he and Schneider knew they had an extraordinary success. The music of *La Belle Hélène* was played all over Paris – on the boulevards and in ballrooms, taverns, and dance halls. Life without care, as proposed in the operetta, was the order of the day in the Second Empire. At 44 years of age, Offenbach was at the height of his success: the king of operetta, the Mozart of the Boulevards.

Then, in 1870, France declared war on Bismarck's Germany, and the tide turned for France and Offenbach. The German Jew who was more French than the French themselves suddenly found himself labeled "a Prussian at heart." By 1873, audiences, tired of social satire, turned to other composers for amusement. Offenbach and his family retreated to their home by the sea at Etretat. Offenbach composed many more operettas, but without the same success, and was soon bankrupt. He toured America, where he was well received, but he missed his family and France. On his return, and in declining health, he worked on the great *Les Contes d'Hoffmann* (The Tales of Hoffmann). Based on stories by E.T.A. Hoffmann, this final work was, at last, Offenbach's entrée into the world of grand opera.

Les Contes is autobiographical in many ways. Like Hoffmann, the narrator of the stories, Offenbach had come to Paris as a poor student who wanted his name to become famous, who sought love and success, money and acclaim. His wishes had been granted. Yet despite his success, he yearned for the respect accredited to Mozart and Rossini. Offenbach had always wanted to compose a work of art, a full-length grand opera, and to do this, at the end of his life, he reached back to his German roots; *Les Contes d'Hoffmann* includes German drinking scenes, a tale of Kleinzach composed in the style of German romanticism, and the great Barcarolle.

Les Contes d'Hoffmann was autobiographical in another, more sobering sense in that it dealt with Offenbach's own death. Even as Antonia, in the opera, knew that to sing would bring about her death, so Offenbach knew that the exertion required to compose this final work would probably kill him. The opera was virtually complete and in rehearsal at the Opéra-Comique, the theatre that had rejected him so many times, when Offenbach died of complications from gout. Many changes and additions were made to the score in Offenbach's absence, but the premiere, in February 1881, was a success. In the end, Offenbach was able to challenge the critics who had patronized him as a composer of mere opéras bouffes with his great final work, an *opéra fantastique* that is found to this day in the repertories of major opera companies worldwide.

Parisian audiences of the 1800s loved their adopted son, while history describes Jacques Offenbach as the composer of the brightest and best French operettas of the time, and of one great *opéra fantastique, Les Contes d'Hoffmann.*

Characters

Hélène, Queen of Sparta	soprano
Menelaus, her husband	tenor buffo
Paris, son of the King of Troy	tenor
Calchas, high priest	baritone
Orestes, son of Agamemnon	mezzo-soprano
Agamemnon	baritone
Achilles, Ajax I, Ajax II, three kings	tenors or baritones
Bacchis, Hélène's maid	soprano

Bibliography

Gammond, Peter, *Offenbach: His Life and Times*, Midas Books, Kent, England, 1980.

Harding, James, *Jacques Offenbach: A Biography*, Riverrun Press, New York, 1980.

Sadie, Stanley, ed., *The Grove Dictionary of Opera*, Macmillan Reference Ltd., London, 1998.

Kátya Kabanová

Leoš Janáček

A ray of light in the realm of darkness.
— Ostrovsky on his play, *The Storm*

Since the premiere of his opera *Jenůfa* in Prague's National Theatre in 1916, Leoš Janáček had been searching for a tragic story on which to base his next opera. He found it in *The Storm* (Groza), by Alexander Ostrovsky. Written in Russia in 1859 and set in Kalinov, a small fictitious town on the banks of the Volga, the play is a classic tale of the individual's struggle against a merciless society. Ostrovsky presents a community ruled by a despotic and self-serving merchant class whose inflexible traditions, prejudices, and hypocrisy keep those less fortunate than themselves at their mercy. Ostrovsky offsets the injustices of this autocratic world with the love story a young woman who refuses to submit to her community, and who, as a result, kills herself in protest. When composing the opera in 1920, Janáček said of Kátya, "The main character is a woman, so gentle by nature, a breeze would carry her away, let alone the storm that breaks over her."

Many facets make up the extraordinary world and art of Leoš Janáček. Born in a small town, Hukvaldy, in 1854 in what was then Moravia, Janáček's musical career was influenced by a wide variety of contemporary composers: Debussy, Mussorgsky, Puccini, Berg, Schoenberg, Stravinsky, and, above all, by Tchaikovsky. Towards the end of the 19th century, Czech music centered round the works of Smetana and Dvořák, composers of works of idealized romanticism in a nationalistic tradition. Janáček's early works reflect these traditions in his compositions of choral songs and his immersion in the folkmusic of his country. Janáček always felt close to nature, and to the people of the land. He said, "In folksong the entire man is enshrined, his body and soul, his milieu, everything. He who is rooted in folksong becomes a complete man."

The young Janáček soon left romanticism behind, however, as he entered his "revolutionary" period in which he spoke with his pen and music against social injustice, defending victims of social and national oppression. His third and final period of compositional style and interest was autobiographical, when, freed from the need to concern himself with national issues following Czech Independence at the end of World War I, he turned his thoughts and creativity to more personal issues. His great operas *Jenůfa*, *Kátya Kabanová*, *The Cunning Little Vixen*, *The Makropoulos Case*, and *From the House of the Dead* all come from an amazing surge of creativity in the final decade of his life.

Janáček's major operas all focus on a woman as the

central character: Jenůfa, Kátya, and later, Emilia Marty of *The Makropoulos Case*. Janáček wrote his own libretto for *Kátya Kabanová*, condensing Ostrovsky's play from five to three acts and cutting much of the social commentary, which was no longer relevant in 1920, after the Russian Revolution. In Janáček's version, Kátya becomes the opera's living, breathing center, and the community in which she lives fades to the periphery – there is not even a true chorus in the opera. He also cut some of the play's characters, leaving the opera with seven leading roles: Kabanicha, the autocratic head of the Kabanov household; her son, Tichon; Kátya, Tichon's wife; Boris, Kátya's lover; the young lovers, Varvara and Kudryash; and Dikoy, a drunken, unscrupulous merchant. Secondary roles include Kuligin, a friend of Kudryash; and two servants, Feklusha and Glasha.

The overture begins with Kátya's music, a gentle *adagio* in the lower strings that is interrupted by the menacing timpani beats of what is called the "Fate" theme, a chilling, insistent motif that recurs often throughout the opera. The music builds to a climax, then lightens with the sound of tinkling sleigh bells, foreshadowing Tichon's departure at the end of Act I. The Fate theme increases the tension once more against a gentle surge of melody from harp and viola d'amore; the latter instrument is used by Janáček throughout the work in connection with Kátya. The battling motifs shift from key to key, until at last Kátya's theme is heard from a mournful English horn, only to be overwhelmed by further disruptive elements of leaping thirds and the Fate theme played fortissimo.

The curtain rises on a sunny day by the banks of the Volga, which on this day is calm and unthreatening. Kudryash, a young intellectual, passes by, singing the river's praises: "What beauty lies in nature." His reverie is interrupted by the sight of Dikoy, the bad-tempered merchant, waving his arms in the air as he bullies his young nephew, Boris. "Lazy rascal," Dikoy shouts, "why do you keep hanging around me?" When Dikoy leaves, Kudryash asks Boris why he stays in the village with his tyrannical uncle. Boris explains that when his parents died in Moscow, he and his sister were left in the guardianship of Dikoy, who has control over their inheritance. For the sake of his sister, Boris feels he must stay in Kalinov with his irascible uncle. This conversation, held on the banks of the Volga, itself a metaphor for the ebb and flow of Russian life, sets the stage for the drama. Already there is a sense of discord; Boris is unhappy; Kudryash, sympathetic to his friend, shrugs his shoulders.

Boris tells Kudryash that he is in love with Tichon's wife, Kátya, and that he waits, hoping to catch a glimpse of her as she returns from church. He expresses his longing to escape the town, and the conflict of his desire for freedom with his love for Kátya, which holds him captive. Kudryash warns him of the dangers of loving a married woman.

Returning from evening service, the Kabanov family appears: Kabanicha, the mother; Varvara, her foster-daughter; Tichon, her son; and Kátya. Kabanicha is angrily telling Tichon he must obey her and go to another town for a while to take charge of the family's business interests there. She criticizes him for placing his wife, Kátya, above her, his mother, in his affections. Tichon tries to placate her as Kátya, in her first lines, quietly assures her mother-in-law, "I respect and honor you just like my own mother. And Tichon loves you as I do." This infuriates the older woman, who orders Kátya to keep quiet. Kátya attempts to defend herself: "Why do you insult me?"

The dialogue between the two women is masterfully

expressed in brisk, irregular, aggressive speech-like bursts from Kabanicha, as she implacably gestures her demands in sharp musical phrases while Kátya stands there, her own music inward-looking and private, fragile and vulnerable. The entrance of Kátya brings to mind the entrance of Madama Butterfly, another fragile heroine, young and at the mercy of the world around her. Janáček wrote of his fascination with Puccini's heroine as he composed his musical portrait of Kátya.

The deceptive peace of the opening scene, disrupted first by Dikoy's outburst and then by the abusive Kabanicha, introduces Kátya as a victim helpless to do much more than acquiesce – behavior appropriate to her role as a young wife living in her mother-in-law's house. When the two women go into the house, Tichon is scolded by Varvara, his foster sister, for not standing up for his wife. Caught between these polarized women, Tichon cannot love both, and dreams of escape the only way he knows: in alcohol.

In the second scene, Kátya and Varvara, close as blood sisters, chatter as they work on their embroidery. In her first long monologue, Kátya imagines how it would be to fly like a bird: "Why can't we spread our wings and fly away?" Varvara is amused but uncomprehending. Kátya reminisces about her happy childhood before coming to the Kabanov house as a bride. Her own mother loved and spoiled her, and she was filled with a love of nature and religion. In the mornings she would bathe in the spring, then bring water for all the flowers. At church, she felt she was in paradise, where "columns of golden light fell from the dome and the incense rose in clouds." In an ecstasy of religious fervor, Kátya imagined angels and heard invisible choirs. As the memory fades, Kátya's mood changes abruptly – now, she tells Varvara, she feels as if she is on the edge of the abyss, "such strange desires are stirring deep in my innermost heart." She tries to resist these desires, but at night in her dreams, she hears, "Someone speaking so tenderly to me, someone embracing me so warmly, calling me to go and live with him." Terrified of the sinfulness of her thoughts, this child of nature, confronted by the religious values on which she has been raised, is trapped. Varvara, who does not understand Kátya's distress, laughs and tries to comfort her.

On the heels of Kátya's confession of her nascent feelings of love for another man (Boris), Tichon enters, ready to leave on his trip. Overcome by fear and guilt, Kátya runs to him and begs him not to go – or, if he must, to take her with him. Tichon doesn't hear the anguish underlying her words. "How can I not go when Mama asks?" he says, and no, he cannot take her with him. In reality, he welcomes the chance to get away from his claustrophobic household for a while. Kátya implores him to make her swear she will not look at another man while he is gone. Tichon, oblivious of her need, blunders, "I cannot ask that of you."

Kabanicha enters: "Tichon, it's time to leave." Sleigh bells announce the waiting troika. Kabanicha insists that Tichon give his wife orders about how to behave in his absence, and dictates a series of commands: "She must respect me, honor me, not stare out of the window, and keep her eyes off other men." Tichon parrots his mother's words – the very words Kátya had asked of him. The victimized Kátya breaks down in tears. "Are you angry with me?" Tichon asks. "No," she replies weakly. "Goodbye." Kabanicha insists that they all sit down together for a moment before departure, a Russian custom that continues to this day. Finally, Kabanicha makes Tichon kneel before her to say farewell, then calls out "Shameless girl" as Kátya throws herself into her husband's arms as he leaves.

Earlier, Kudryash had warned Boris that "Kabanicha is a hypocrite, full of alms and charity, but inside the house she wields a rod of iron," and in this scene of domesticity behind the walls of the Kabanov house the horror of the family relationships is graphically revealed. Tichon is a mere pawn; Kabanicha hates and resents Kátya; only the lively Varvara, aware of Kátya's pain, is sympathetic toward her. Kabanicha senses Kátya's restlessness and guilty longing when she demands that Tichon make his wife swear she will not look at another man. Both women fear the outcome of such an event, but for very different reasons. The music between Tichon and Kátya doesn't connect, revealing the lack of understanding between husband and wife. Tichon's deafness to Kátya's despair exacerbates her fears of what will happen if he leaves. When he ignores her, she is cut adrift, tossed about like a bird in a storm.

In Act II, which is set sometime later, Kátya has regained her composure. The three women sew together in the confined space of the living area of Kabanicha's house. Kabanicha nags at Kátya and wants to know why she did not wail, as was the custom, when Tichon left. Kátya responds that she does not believe in a public display of grief. When Kabanicha leaves, Varvara excitedly tells Kátya that she has arranged for them to sleep in the summerhouse together – not only that, she has taken the key to the garden gate, implying that they can leave the house anytime they want. Kátya is terrified of the key and its implications. "I cannot take it," she cries. "Keep it. Don't tempt me." Varvara places the key on the table and runs off. Kátya struggles with her conscience. "Sin and shame, I should throw the key in the river." Instead, her hand reaches for the key, picks it up, and puts it in her pocket as she rationalizes, "What's the harm in just speaking to him? Fate has willed it so. I will see Boris."

Kátya leaves the room as Kabanicha enters, followed by the drunken Dikoy. He describes how he beat a servant when the man asked to be paid, then felt sorry for his behavior and begged the servant for forgiveness on his knees, which is where he finds himself now, in front of Kabanicha. He whines to the stern woman; she pushes him away. Janáček's music suggests that a sadomasochistic relationship exists between this ugly pair, in sharp contrast to the love relationships of the young couples.

A musical interlude brings us to the celebrated double love scene, which echoes a similar one in Tchaikovsky's *Eugene Onegin*: the serious couples, Onegin/Tatyana and Kátya/Boris, are balanced by the lighter, more carefree pair, Olga/Lensky and Varvara/Kudryash.

The music sets us down outside the gate to the Kabanovs' garden; a path leads to the river, a little way off. Kudryash sings himself a little folk tune as he waits for Varvara, but it is Boris who first appears – he has been told by "some girl or other" to come to the gate for a secret rendezvous. Kudryash once again warns him of the danger of loving Kátya, a married woman, but Boris is in love, so the two men wait. Varvara opens the gate, singing a folk tune in answer to Kudryash's call, and whispers to Boris that Kátya is on her way. She takes Kudryash by the arm, and the lovers walk off into the shadows. Kátya now approaches, nervous, frightened, unsure of herself, and ready for flight at a moment's notice. Boris reassures her, tells her he loves her, and she soon sinks into his arms. He holds her as she sings, "Now I may die happy."

Varvara returns to suggest that Boris and Kátya go for a stroll together by the river. The couples change places when Varvara and Kudryash return as Boris and Katya stroll away arm in arm. The two love duets intertwine, the folk theme of the younger couple contrasting with the offstage ecstasy of the doomed love of Boris and Kátya. Finally, Kudryash calls the lovers back as dawn appears on the horizon. Kudryash and Varvara part playfully, while Boris and Kátya bid one another a passionate goodnight in long-held, wafting phrases that recall the final bars of Madama Butterfly and Pinkerton's love duet.

Act III catapults us from the languor of the closing bars of Act II to the menacing sounds of a storm in which thunder, rain, and the river become the forces directing the action. In a somewhat surreal scenario, all the main characters, blown about by the storm, take refuge in a ruined building whose walls reveal a faded fresco of the eternal fires of hell. Waiting in the ruin for the storm to abate, Dikoy and Kudryash argue about the usefulness of lightning rods. Dikoy insists that storms are sent as punishments from God. As the rain eases, Varvara comes running to Boris on the other side of the stage: "What are we to do with Kátya?" she asks breathlessly. "Tichon has returned, Kátya is distraught, and Kabanicha watches her like a serpent. She is so pale and shaking. She wanders through the house like a madwoman." Boris is at a loss to know what to do. Finally Kátya appears, terrified of the storm and the turmoil in her soul. Catching sight of Boris she cries out: "Does he care so little for my suffering?" Varvara tries to calm the panicked woman as the storm builds once again. When Kabanicha and Tichon appear, Kátya, no longer able to deal with the terror in her heart, falls to her knees. "Mama, Tichon, look on this sinner and pity her." She confesses to having spent every night with Boris since Tichon's departure. Kátya collapses for a moment into Tichon's arms, then runs off wildly into the darkness of the stormy night.

Some hours later, Varvara and Kudryash meet on the riverbank. Kabanicha has threatened to lock Varvara in the house, but she has managed to escape. The two plan to leave at once for Moscow.

In the turmoil of this menacing night, the voices of men are heard in the distance as they search and call out "Katerina." Slowly, forlornly, Kátya enters alone, seeking Boris. "I have brought shame and ruin on myself and on him." She hears the voices calling her, "like funeral voices chanting." She recalls that a woman like herself would be thrown in the river for her adultery, that Kabanicha said she should be buried alive – but Kátya wants to live to atone her sins. Her wandering monologue expresses her inability to return to the harsh brutality of the Kabanov household, her despair at the thought of being incarcerated once more, her loss of Boris. She longs for death, and for Boris. She calls to him, "Answer me, answer me!"

Hearing her cry, Boris appears, runs to her and holds her close in a musical embrace beyond words. This is the most touching moment in the opera; in it, we empathize fully with the tortured Kátya, her simultaneous longing for love and her guilt, her need for freedom and her imprisonment. She tells Boris she meant him no harm. He tells her his uncle is sending him away to Siberia, where he must go alone and where "I shall be free to do as I wish." Kátya says her mother-in-law will torture her, people will mock her, Tichon will beat her when he is drunk. Then she remembers what she wanted to tell him. "Give alms to each beggar you meet. Ask them to pray for my soul." The stage directions at this point instruct the offstage chorus to intone a vowel between U and O, like the Volga sighing, as Boris tears himself away, leaving Kátya to listen to the song of the river. She is calm as she walks to its side. Underscored by soft, ominous beats from the timpani, her last words, as she falls into the dark river, reveal her acceptance of death: "Birds will sing as they fly above me where I am buried, flowers will blossom there. So peaceful, so lovely, and I must die."

In the dim light, someone sees Kátya fall, and a crowd quickly gathers, carrying lanterns. Dikoy pulls her body from the cold waters and lays her at the feet of Kabanicha and Tichon. The despairing Tichon turns on his mother: "You are the one who killed her, you and you alone." Kabanicha pulls herself up and coldly addresses the crowd, "I must thank you, friends and neighbors, for your kindness," as Tichon throws himself on the body of his wife. The curtain falls to the sound of the Volga's sighing voice, and the relentless beats of the Fate theme on the timpani.

So ends *Kátya Kabanová* and the story of a young woman whose purity and innocence was savaged by the ruthless community in which she was forced to live. Kátya was a triple victim: of her mean-spirited and jealous mother-in-law; of Tichon and Boris, the weak men who would not stand up for her; and of her own sense of religious guilt, which led directly to her confession and death.

Musically, *Kátya Kabanová* is gripping and intense, and holds one rapt in the emotion of the moment from start to finish. Janáček writes consciously of the now. "The art of dramatic writing," he once said, "is to compose a melodic curve which will, as if by magic, reveal immediately a human being in one definite phase of his existence." Janáček objectively presents what his characters are thinking and feeling without indulging them or becoming sentimental. He stands, brilliantly, "midway between classical impersonality and romantic involvement with his subjects," as Michael Ewans so eloquently puts it. His music somehow describes, simultaneously, a musical balance between freedom and relentless control; words and music are crystallized in a moment of time. Kátya's monologues are clear examples of this approach: Kátya and audience alike are caught up in the immediacy of her dreams and predicament. Janáček's heroines are not mad; they are aware of their actions and the consequences of those actions. Kátya accepts without hesitation the fact that her death is inevitable. It simply happens, as it must.

Over the years, Janáček developed what he called "speech melody," a technique that depicts living speech in all its regional and individual idiosyncrasies, catching the moment or a certain emotion. Kátya and Kabanicha are differentiated musically by their speech patterns, by types of sounds and word settings, and by type of voice: Kátya's soprano against Kabanicha's contralto. As Kátya and Kabanicha are set apart by their respective musics, Varvara and Kudryash are joined by the repetitive, circular folksongs they sing to one another, alternating verses and harmonies. Boris and Tichon are never fully described in the music – both function as satellites of Kátya, existing only because of and/or in relation to her. Both are weak: Tichon is controlled by his mother; Boris offers Kátya little support, and leaves her when the storm breaks.

Janáček was in his late sixties when *Kátya Kabanová* premiered in Brno in 1921; the productivity of his final decade of life is astounding. Three pivotal events brought about this amazing surge of creativity: after years of struggle to be recognized and get his works produced in major opera houses, *Jenůfa* was finally presented at Prague's National Theatre, quickly establishing Janáček as the heir to Dvořák and Smetana, and as Czechoslovakia's leading opera composer in his own right. Second, with the birth of the Czech Republic, political pressure was lifted from Janáček and many European composers, who could now return to a more normal way of life following the years of struggle and deprivation of World War I.

The third and most important event of Janáček's later years took place in 1917, when he met Kamila Stösslová. She was 25 and married, he was 63 and unhappily married. From the time they met until his death, Janáček's love for Kamila inspired him – she was his muse and inspiration. Their relationship was one of friendship at a distance, for Kamila cared little for his music and remained true to her marriage. He wrote her more than 700 letters; few of hers to him have survived. Janáček wrote to her, "During the writing of *Kátya*, I needed to know a great, measureless love. . . . I always placed your image on Kátya. . . . Her love went a different way, but nevertheless it was a great, beautiful love!" Janáček told Kamila repeatedly that she was the inspiration not only for *Kátya*, a woman who has an affair in her husband's absence, but also for *The Cunning Little Vixen* (1923), which describes a resourceful and self-sacrificing wife and mother, and for *The Makropoulos Affair* (1925), with its 300-year-old woman whom everyone loves but who loves no one.

Though he begged Kamila to come to the premieres of his operas, she never did. The works he dedicated to her, including *Kátya Kabanová*, and the scores he sent her, were barely acknowledged. In the end, however, by a strange course of events, Kamila was with him when, at age 74, he died in the town of his birth, Hukvaldy, in 1928.

Critic Desmond Shaw-Taylor wrote, "The most striking thing about *Kátya Kabanová* is the undiluted strength and purity of its feeling. The amazingly pregnant melodic germs frequently build into ample, flowing phrases. These brief germs spread like a thought in the mind with all sorts of new and expressive harmonies. Janáček is like those rare people

whose unselfconscious honesty of mind makes us ashamed
of exaggeration or pretense."

Characters

Dikoy, a rich merchant	bass
Boris Grigoryevich, his nephew	tenor
Marfa Kabanová, Kabanicha, a rich widow	contralto
Tichon, her son	tenor
Kátya Kabanová, Tichon's wife	soprano
Varvara, Kabanicha's foster daughter	mezzo-soprano
Kudryash, Varvara's lover	tenor
Kuligin, friend of Kudryash	baritone
Glasha and Feklusha, servants	mezzo-sopranos

Bibliography

Ewans, Michael, *Janáček's Tragic Operas*, Faber and Faber Ltd., London 1977.

John, Nicolas, ed., *Janáček: Jenůfa/Kátya Kabanová*, English National Opera Guide 33, Riverrun Press, New York, 1985.

Tausky, Vilem and Margaret, eds., *Janáček: Leaves from his Life*, Kahn and Averill, London, 1982.

Tyrrell, John, ed., *Leoš Janáček: Káťa Kabanová*, Cambridge Opera Handbook, Cambridge University Press, 1982.

Vogel, Jaroslav, *Leoš Janáček: A Biography*, Orbis Publishing, London, 1981.

Madame Mao

Bright Sheng

Chinese and Asian music is unquestionably
my mother tongue, while I consider
Western music culture my father tongue.
— Bright Sheng

Sheng Zong-Liang was born in Shanghai in 1955, at the
height of Mao Zedong's supreme leadership of the vast
country that is the People's Republic of China. Sheng first
studied music with his mother at the age of four but, Sheng
recalls, "When I was 11, the Cultural Revolution came and
our piano was taken away. One day I got music-sick and
sneaked into the junior high classroom to play the school
piano." Junior high was the highest level of education
permitted by Mao. When Sheng was 15, he, along with the

majority of China's youth, was sent away from home to be re-educated by the peasants (in those days, most young Chinese were forced to become farmers). Because Madame Mao, wife of Mao Zedong, was interested in the piano and western romantic harmonies, she became, ironically, the means whereby the young Sheng became a musician. Because of his musical abilities, he was allowed to join a folk song and dance group as a percussionist and pianist. His destination was the distant Province of Qinghai, on the China-Tibet border, where the folk group was managed by the provincial government.

Sheng was to spend seven and a half years in Qinghai. He describes the land of his exile as "a basically inhospitable place with a harsh climate, situated on the Tibetan-Qinghai plateau and called 'the roof of the world.' One of the poorest regions in China, Qinghai is populated by many immigrants and has several distinct cultures – such as Tibetan, Chinese Muslim, Mongolian, and Russian Cossack, in addition to the Chinese. The ethnic backgrounds of the people were rich, but their lives were poor. Life was tough. Their only entertainment was singing folk songs. In Qinghai there is a special kind of folk song called *hau'er*, or flower song, which everyone sang in the provincial dialect of Chinese. The people all lived close to each other; there was no ethnic tension or fighting." Many of Sheng's later compositions found their source in these lovely flower songs.

With no teachers in Qinghai, Sheng had to teach himself, imitating others by watching them play. "I would watch and listen to other people when I visited other cities, and learned to grasp quickly whatever they were doing that might be helpful to me as a musician," he says. "It was a very good habit. One is always one's own best teacher. Later I conducted and, after a while, I began to arrange music."

Sheng returned home when the Cultural Revolution ended in 1976, and in 1978 became one of the first students to be accepted into the newly re-opened Shanghai Conservatory of Music. He was not happy there. "They didn't know anything about Chinese music. They were writing 12-tone music in the avant-garde style of the 1960s." This was to be Sheng's first struggle between the Eastern and Western styles that he would strive to combine in later years. He describes the dilemma: "Chinese music is meant for the performer's self-indulgence, not for entertainment. The philosophy behind the music is that it is a way to cultivate yourself, a way to soothe your mind and spirit. In Chinese music the rhythm is not notated, the music is not meant to be reduplicated at other performances, as rhythms in Western music are."

Bright Sheng's family name, Sheng, means "something like 'bright lights.' " After reading a book that referred to an Englishman as Mr. Bright, Sheng took "Bright" as his first name when he came to the United States, in 1982. On arriving in New York, Sheng studied at Queens College and Columbia University with Leonard Bernstein and America's leading teachers and composers, earning graduate degrees in composition and conducting. In the course of his studies and work in subsequent years, Sheng continued to pursue his dream of bringing the elements of Eastern and Western music together, something his professors advised him not to do. "I am a mixture of not only East and West but of Tibetan and Chinese within the East. Why shouldn't my music reflect that? People acknowledge 'artistic license;' I embrace 'cultural license' – the right to reflect my appreciation and understanding of both cultures in my work. You can either struggle with cultural identity or make good advantage of it." When Sheng studied with Bernstein at Tanglewood, Bernstein reinforced the young composer's dream, telling him, "Everything is fusion." Sheng's dream became reality when, in November 2001, he was awarded the prestigious MacArthur Foundation Fellowship, which described him as "a fresh voice in cross-cultural music."

Sheng's career has been meteoric. His *H'un (Lacerations): In Memoriam 1966–78* was composed as an orchestral portrait of the Cultural Revolution in 1988. This haunting work evokes the terror of the Revolution in music that paraphrases William Blake's *Songs of Innocence and Experience* – the innocence of a boy growing up as an exile in the years of the Revolution, of leaving folk song and a beloved country behind, alongside the experience and sophistication of a well-trained composer who honed his craft in the West. Sheng is also an active conductor and pianist, and has served as artistic advisor to some of America's leading orchestras.

Sheng's one-act opera, *The Song of Majnun*, was written while he was the resident conductor with the Lyric Opera of Chicago, from 1989 to 1992. *Majnun* brought Sheng back to his Asian roots in his telling of the tale of Majnun and Layla, a young couple who fall in love but are forbidden by Layla's family to be together. Majnun's grief drives him to the point of madness, and he sings of his lost love in a song that travels the country, until it comes to Layla's ears. The lovers attempt to meet, but it is not to be. Layla dies of a broken heart as Majnun dreams of a tree in which perches a bird carrying a jewel in its beak. The bird drops the jewel into Majnun's hands at the moment of Layla's death; the jewel is her tear.

Sheng explains, "In *H'un* I tried to describe the terror of the Revolution by building the entire work on the tuneless, dissonant interval of a minor second. In *Three Chinese Love Songs* [for voice, piano and viola], I told of my affection for the beauty of melodies and simple consonant harmonies. *Majnun* provided a perfect opportunity to explore both sides within one composition." The Asian legend made it possible for Sheng to use the language of oriental harmonies. The character of Majnun also interested him for the degradation the young man suffered at the hands of his society, which forced him to become alienated and isolated, not unlike Berg's Wozzeck. "On one level, *Majnun* is autobiographical, telling a love story between China and me."

The Silver River, a multicultural music-theatre tale of two more star-crossed lovers, was first presented in Santa Fe in 1997, reworked in collaboration with director Ong Keng Sen, and presented, with enormous success, at New York's Lincoln Center Festival in the summer of 2002. Based on a Chinese fable, *The Silver River* tells of the beautiful Goddess-Weaver who falls in love with a mortal, Cowherd, to the annoyance of her father, the Jade Emperor. The Golden Buffalo brings the lovers together, but then is commanded to separate them. Sheng says, "This is not strictly an opera in Western terms, because there are other elements in it – operatic vocal writing, Chinese opera, a speaking role, and dance."

Now, in 2003, Bright Sheng is busily preparing for two premieres: a quadruple concerto for the New York Philharmonic in the spring, featuring Yo-Yo Ma and Emanuel Ax, and his new full-length opera, *Madame Mao*, for The Santa Fe Opera in July and August.

Jiang Qing: Woman of History *

In *Madame Mao: The White-Boned Demon*, Ross Terrill tells the horrendous story of the life of Jiang Qing, the woman who rose from nothing to wield phenomenal power as the wife of Chairman Mao Zedong. She was the main instigator of the Cultural Revolution in the 1960s and '70s, was condemned as a member of the notorious Gang of Four following Mao's death, and committed suicide in 1991.

Madame Mao, first named Shumeng, was born in 1914 to a father of the landlord class and a mother who was her father's concubine. Mother and daughter were soon cast out of the family to fend for themselves; Shumeng's mother became a domestic servant, and Shumeng was raised by her maternal grandparents in Jinan. At 14, she joined her first theatre group, reveling in the freedom theatre provided her young, independent spirit. She studied briefly at the Arts Academy and acted in what were called "anti-feudal" plays. Now calling herself Yunhe, she played her first Nora in Ibsen's *The Doll's House* at the Academy, a role that took on extraordinary meaning for her for the rest of her life. Yunhe saw herself as Nora, the trapped woman, forced to be subservient to a man while longing to break down the walls of the doll's house that confined her. In 1930, at age 16, she married Fei, a graduate student. The marriage lasted only a few months. The aspiring actress went to Qingdao to seek her fortune, got a job as a library clerk at the University, and took classes. She met her second husband Yu Qiwei who was a passionate Communist and, in this environment, she too joined the Chinese Communist Party.

* There are numerous ways of spelling Chinese names in English. For clarity, I have used Jiang Qing rather than Chiang Ch'ing or Jiang Ching (as in the libretto) for Madame Mao, and He Zizhen rather than ZiZheng (as in the libretto) for Mao's former wife.

When Yu Qiwei chose the Party over Yunhe, this marriage came to an end. Yunhe packed her bags once more and moved to Shanghai, a wildly hedonistic city that was a crossroads for business in the East. It was in Shanghai that Yunhe became Lan Ping, a known actress of stage and film. She took risks by dabbling in politics, but at heart she was more interested in promoting herself than in serving the Party. At 20, she found her greatest success when she played Nora for the second time.

Lan Ping had been adrift and alone since her second divorce, but in Shanghai she met an art critic called named Tang Na, lived with and married him in what was to be a tempestuous relationship. Lan Ping never accepted the role of wife easily; marriage interfered with her ideas of personal freedom. This third marriage ultimately foundered, and, in May 1937, Lan Ping and Tang Na were divorced. Japan's attack on Shanghai later that summer put an end to work in films and the theatre; Lan Ping moved once again and found herself in Yanan, where the leaders of China's communist guerrillas were living in caves. Their leader was Mao Zedong.

Lan Ping soon came to the attention of the attractive Mao, and the two began a passionate relationship: the actress was 25, the rising leader 45. In those months, Mao was ending his third marriage, to He Zizhen. Zizhen had been Mao's political ally through hard years of physical struggle, but now their relationship was ending in bitterness. He Zizhen was sent away to a sanatorium in the Soviet Union, and Mao was free to flirt with whomever he chose. He and Lan Ping, now renamed Jiang Qing (Green River), were married in 1939. The Communist Party was not happy about this liaison, permitting it only on the condition that Jiang Qing agreed to devote herself to looking after Mao, and to refrain from any political activity for 30 years. For the time being, Jiang accepted dependence as Mao's wife, as the mother of his children, and occasionally as his assistant. Many years later, however, the time bomb exploded, and the smoldering woman wreaked vengeance on those who had muzzled her at the time of her marriage.

But for now, in Yanan, Jiang Qing appeared to abide by the rules, and played the role of dutiful wife through the 1940s and '50s. Mao was fascinated by Jiang in the early years of their relationship, but, as time passed, he had many other affairs. Publicly, he alternately supported Jiang and denigrated her. As his power grew, she remained doggedly by his side, the wife of Chairman Mao. Jiang was aware of every political move made by Mao and his colleagues. She said nothing when Mao decreed that the arts must serve only the cause of communism. In 1949, the Chinese Communist Party wrested control from Chiang Kai-Shek, and Mao became the Supreme Leader of China. In these momentous months in Mao's life his wife Jiang, like He Zizhen before her, was confined by the Party to a Soviet sanatorium, with Mao's concurrence.

When Mao began to reshape the cultural life of China, Jiang was appointed to a Film Guidance committee to evaluate films. In this position, she used her newfound influence as a step up the ladder to personal political power. Though battling illness, Jiang gradually built a power base in the early 1960s. She took control of her life, made an amazing recovery, and returned to live with Mao in Beijing, the capital and the seat of power. With Mao's support, she focused her energies on the theatre, decreeing that Chinese theatre could present no plays written before the 1920s. "Make it revolutionary or ban it," Jiang insisted. She took control of Chinese dance-drama groups, introducing communist themes and creating political operas and ballets, making the dancers live in army units so they could better interpret war and class hatred. She gained control of radio and influenced the press, who wrote of the new operas and ballets, "They are shining pearls of proletarian literature and art, fostered personally by Comrade Jiang Qing. They sparkle with the thoughts of Mao Zedong." In 1966 she was appointed chief advisor to the army on dance, ballet, and novels.

Mao, who was losing power in the early 1960s, now found his wife an able ally. He fought back against his enemies by rallying 11 million Red Guards, primarily students, to rebel against the bureaucracy, destroying "outdated" and "counter-revolutionary" symbols and values. The old ways were indeed destroyed, and the masses applauded Mao and Jiang. The Cultural Revolution was underway. Oddly, pianos, which should have been condemned as "bourgeois" instruments, survived the Revolution thanks to Jiang Qing, who viewed the piano as being, like herself, individualistic. With the success of the Cultural Revolution, the struggling actress and the frustrated housewife of the 1950s could move toward vengeance as the strong political force she became in the '60s. In a personal vendetta, she ruined the careers of thousands of officials and performing artists, using the Red Guards as her personal army. Anyone who questioned her actions ended up in prison, or worse. The vast audiences to whom she spoke believed that she spoke for Mao. "I bring you greetings from Chairman Mao," she would begin her talks. Her fiercely independent spirit, her enormous energy, and her determination to succeed at all costs found vindication and release in the horror that was the Cultural Revolution.

At last, in the 1970s, with China in chaos, Mao realized

that the time for rebellion was coming to an end and that his masses would have to unite. By this time, Jiang, along with other political friends and foes, turned their thoughts to naming Mao's successor. Jiang began to see herself as China's leader, taking as her model the Empress Wu, who had lived 1300 years earlier. Like Jiang, Wu had started out humbly, as a concubine to the Emperor Gao Zong. She gained great power by replacing the Emperor's first wife and involving herself in politics. Wu bore the Emperor two sons, and maintained a highly erotic relationship with him while running the empire behind the scenes. At the Emperor's death she took full control of China, going so far as to kill her own sons when they threatened her position. She titled herself, "Holy Mother Divine Imperial One."

There are many parallels between Wu's and Jiang's rise to power – up to the point of their husbands' deaths. Emulating Wu, Jiang defied every rule in the book in the effort to become China's leader, when it was universally understood that no woman could become the supreme leader of China, and no woman could be at the forefront of politics. None of this deterred Jiang. She began to surround herself with her own supporters, in particular with three hard-core communists who came to be known, along with Jiang, as the Gang of Four.

As Mao weakened physically, he distanced himself from Jiang. In 1974 he wrote to her, "It's better not to see each other. You haven't carried out many of the things I talked to you about over the years." At 81, Mao was old and ill, with little fight left, though no one dared oppose him as long as he lived. In February 1976, in an effort to improve relations with America, President and Mrs. Nixon were invited to Beijing and taken to the theatre by Jiang, a moment of history enshrined in composer John Adams's opera *Nixon in China.*

Mao died in September of that year. He was succeeded not by Jiang, his wife of 38 years, but by a political outsider, Hua Guofeng. A month after Mao's death, Hua Guofeng had Jiang and the Gang of Four arrested. The indictment charged the Four on two counts: for persecuting leaders, intellectuals, and ordinary people; and for trying to usurp the power of the Party and the state. Cartoons appeared depicting Jiang as a witch or a rat feeding on the picked-clean bones of her victims; she came to be called "the white-boned demon."

Jiang's trial, in 1980, was a show trial that served as revenge for those she had destroyed during the Cultural Revolution. At 66, she was well-groomed and ready to play her last role; she entered the courtroom like Marie Antoinette, a queen wrongly accused, defying her judges: "If I am guilty, how about you all?" "Shut up, Jiang Qing," was the unanimous response. Contrary to communist tradition, Jiang never confessed, and the trial ended in chaos. The verdict was "Guilty on all counts, a sentence of death, suspended for two years to see how she behaves." The Party could not afford to turn Mao's widow into a martyr. In prison, she sewed dolls and wrote defiant statements. Eleven years after her trial, at the age of 77 and living under house arrest, Jiang Qing hung herself, thus ending the extraordinary era in China of Mao Zedong and Jiang Qing.

Madame Mao: The Opera

The foregoing is the story that composer Bright Sheng and celebrated librettist and director Colin Graham have transformed into an opera. Sheng writes, "We wrote this opera based loosely on the life of Jiang Qing and we did change a great deal to make it dramatically more compelling as opposed to being historically correct. It is an art work." One must keep this in mind when approaching a creative work based on the life of a real person. It is tempting to mistakenly "learn" her story through art rather than historical fact.

Of greater interest is Bright Sheng's approach to the subject matter, and his musical blending of East and West. (The opera includes scenes of stylized Chinese Opera. The libretto is sung in English). Sheng and Graham chose an intriguing way of bringing Madame Mao to life: The seven scenes of Act I move backward in time, from her death to her early days as an actress. Act II, in eight scenes, moves forward, from Jiang's first encounter with Mao, through the Cultural Revolution, to Mao's death and Jiang's own imprisonment and suicide. The approach is effective, since Jiang's story is not widely familiar to Western audiences; thus, while the journey back in time is informative, her life becomes much more clearly understood on the return journey.

The set is stark, without frills; the costumes are the drab shirts and baggy pants dictated by the Party dress code. The Accusers act as a recurring motif throughout the opera. Their chairs are moved from place to place during the action, sometimes with people sitting in them, other times not, giving the impression that the Accusers are always present.

Madame Mao/Jiang Qing is played by two singers: a lyric soprano plays Jiang in her 20s, and a mezzo-soprano plays the older Jiang. There are four other principals: Mao, Zizhen (Mao's former wife), an Actor, and an Actress. Completing the cast are the eight Accusers, a chorus of 24, and eight dancers.

Following the Prelude, a body is seen upstage, swinging on a rope made of handkerchiefs and sheets. The older Jiang enters and observes, "I rose from obscurity to fame, and in death I still survive. Let me dissect myself before you." The scene fades to her trial and the Accusers: "Jiang Qing, you are accused of crimes against humanity. Confess, confess, confess." Jiang defends herself: "I am the wife of Mao Zedong." "Shut up, shut up," the Accusers cry. The libretto uses the reported words of the 1980 trial.

The trial scene fades back in time as Jiang assures Mao that she will finish his plan when he is gone. Mao laughs ironically; "Always so ready to seize the crown – you see yourself as the cruel Empress Wu." Jiang, the actress, replies, "I am the only one to play that part." She tells him she will try to find out who is right, "The world or I . . . ," in words that echo Nora, as the scene shifts further back in time to the young Jiang playing the Ibsen role. Jiang is seen surrounded by adoring men, who drop her, one by one. She is accused of using her bourgeois charms to flaunt her promiscuity. "You battle on the stage for sex, money and the power of men," the Accusers insist. A stylized ballroom dance re-creates Jiang's liaisons with her husbands: "A moon-struck fan, an ambitious revolutionary and an actor who adored me." The dancing stops when the Actor tells Jiang she will not be Nora in his film. The young Jiang cries out, "Shameful to be born a woman, beaten, abused, betrayed by all you men." She reminisces about her childhood; her exhausted mother, who sang lullabies to her; her first acting experiences in "a world of Golden Boys and girls of Silver Sky."

The act ends when the older Jiang rises to her feet and declares, as Mao is seen advancing with his troops to climactic music and bright lights: "China shall make herself again, One man reaches up to save her soul."

Act II opens with traditional Chinese Opera, in the retelling of the story of Empress Wu's rise to power. The

Emperor, called General Gao, and sung by Mao, strikes a pose. The role of the Empress, sung by Zizhen, Mao's former wife, enters, saying she will defend her husband. They dance together until the concubine Liu/Wu, who is sung by Jiang, appears with her warriors and separates the couple. As Liu/Wu sings "Gao shall be my own," a battle ensues. It ends when Gao takes the side of Liu/Wu.

The scene moves from Chinese Opera and picks up the story in the present day as Mao approaches, touches, and disrobes Jiang, saying, "I need an extraordinary woman whose charm and beauty fire my soul." In the duet that follows, Jiang and Mao make love until Zizhen, his wife, appears at the door of Mao's cave, cursing them both. In a replay of the ancient story, the women fight, until Mao commands the guards to take Zizhen away.

The Accusers, representatives of the Communist Party, argue with Mao: "How can you abandon your wife for an actress, a creature from the gutter?" But Mao insists he wants Jiang as his wife. Finally, the Committee agrees, on condition that Jiang "devotes her life to the welfare of our Leader, refrains from political action and never appears [in public] as your wife." Mao agrees, as Jiang seethes inwardly: "Again the prey of men, victim of their power."

In the Dance of Life that follows, Mao dances with four Beauties, ignoring Jiang, torturing her by singing the words of their love duet to the passing Beauties. When he leaves, Jiang pulls herself together and resolves, "Our love may have rotted away, but revenge is born in my heart." As the scene shifts back to Chinese Opera once more, we see the Emperor take Liu as his Empress. She murmurs, "For 30 years I've waited for my chance and will subdue the people to my will." Suddenly, Liu's soldiers are replaced by Red Guards and the Emperor by Mao as Jiang cries out, "A Cultural Revolution

shall cauterize society and sanitize our lives!" The Accusers
remind her that her policies have "caused the hatred, pain
and death of 30 million souls."

Harsh, discordant music describes the punishment of
Jiang's victims as they are dragged before her by the Red
Guards, pleading for their lives, but the merciless Jiang
pronounces a death sentence on them all. The victims cry
out as the chorus chants, "White-boned demon, white-
boned demon." Jiang: "Everything I did, Mao told me to – I
was his dog – if he said 'Bite,' I bit."

But now Mao lies on his deathbed, wondering about
Jiang Qing, who "Blindly struts her hour upon the stage,
imagining she can outwit them all." Jiang reminds him that
through all the challenges of their years together she stood
by him. But Mao has had enough. "I want no more of you."
In a trio, Zizhen returns from her asylum to mock Mao,
who angrily dismisses both women. The infuriated Jiang
cries out, "For 30 years I've waited for this chance to crown
my life as I deserve." But for Jiang, the outcome was not to
be the same as for Empress Wu.

At her trial, where the opera began, the chorus
continues to chant "White-boned demon" as Jiang defends
herself, accusing the judges of being the People's enemies.
Pandemonium results, and Jiang is removed from the court
by the guards.

Finally alone, the younger and older Jiangs wonder,
"We'll see who's right, the world or I," as they gaze up at the
swinging rope.

So ends the story of Jiang Qing, woman of history, wife of
Mao Zedong, the Supreme Leader of China, and instigator
with him of the purge that was the Cultural Revolution,
destroyer of countless millions of men and women. She is
remembered – lest we forget – in the biography of Ross

Terrill in his *Madame Mao: The White-Boned Demon*, in the insightful libretto of Colin Graham, and, above all, in this evocative opera by Chinese composer Bright Sheng.

Characters

Jiang Qing I (Madame Mao)	dramatic mezzo-soprano
Jiang Qing II (Madame Mao in her 20s)	lyric soprano
Mao Zedong	baritone
Zizhen, Mao's former wife	mezzo-soprano
The Actor	tenor
The Actress	soprano
The Accusers	6 male & 2 female soloists

Bibliography

I am grateful to Ross Terrill for his book, *Madame Mao: The White-Boned Demon*, a major source of information in the section on the life of Jiang Qing. His book is carefully researched and well-referenced.
Terrill, Ross, *Madame Mao: The White-Boned Demon*, Stanford University Press, CA, 1999.
"Bright Sheng, Composer," *Michigan Today*, Fall 1998, University of Michigan, www.umich.edu/~newsinfo/MT/98/mt13f98.
"Bright Sheng: Biography," www.schirmer.com/composers/sheng_bio.
Graham, Colin, *Madame Mao* libretto, G. Schirmer Inc., New York, 2003.
Kerner, Leighton, *H'un (Lacerations)*, liner note, New World Records 780407-2, 1991.
Kozinn, Allan, "A Composer Who Combines Musical Styles Worlds Apart," *The New York Times* on the Web, July 16, 2002, www.nytimes.com/2002/07/16/arts/music/16sh.
Sheng, Bright, "Two essays by Bright Sheng: 'How I Came to Be a Composer' and 'My Biggest Challenge,' " www.schirmer.com/composers/sheng_essay2.

Further Reading

Witke, Roxane, *Comrade Chiang Ch'ing*, Little Brown & Co., Boston, 1977. (In 1972, Jiang Qing, aka Chiang Ch'ing, gave an exclusive series of interviews to the American scholar and biographer Roxane Witke, much to Mao's annoyance.)

Madame Mao was commissioned by The Santa Fe Opera; excerpts from the libretto by Colin Graham used by permission from G. Schirmer, Inc.

Sentences for Jiang Qing
by William Slaughter

Jiang Qing
one of the gang
Mao's widow
his fourth wife
who never really
lived with him
after Liberation
in 1949
has outlived
herself
is ready to die
but life for her
goes on for her
in Qin Cheng
a prison not far
from Beijing
where she has
a room of her own
but not much
is left for her
not movies not
lovers not China
only rag dolls
she sews
for children
she never sees
knowing that
face in China
is self is pride

and saving it
a career
I wonder
if before she
sews the buttons
on for eyes
the smiling
mouth the nose
those dolls
she ever sees
a child's face
her own face
innocent
and confesses
all at once
her guilt
how without
intending to
she became
the Chairman's dog
when he told her
to bite she bit
and just
for a second
regretted it
all her country
men and women
hurt lost
gone dead

Reprinted by permission of the poet, William Slaughter, and excerpted from his book, *The Politics of My Heart*, Pleasure Boat Studio Press, New York, 1996

Così fan tutte

Wolfgang Amadeus Mozart

Nothing's perfect here below!
      – Don Alfonso

*C*osì fan tutte has challenged audiences from the day of its premiere at Vienna's Burgtheater in January 1790. Audiences were amused by the plot – the premise for the opera came, supposedly, from a Viennese scandal in which two sisters switched fiancés when their lovers pursued them in disguise. The Emperor Joseph, amused by the incident, asked Mozart and Da Ponte to write an opera about it. The idea of infidelity as the basis of an opera plot was hardly new; an older source was the story of Cephalus and Procris, from Ovid's *Metamorphosis*, in which a man disguises himself in order to test his wife's fidelity. Another source was a play by Ariosto, *Orlando Furioso*, from 1516, in which two young men, on discovering that their wives are unfaithful, go off on a journey. Learning that all women are susceptible, (*Così fan tutte*, All women are like that) they return contentedly to their wives.

Così fan tutte is a choreographed *dramma giocosa*, (the librettist's term), or *opéra buffa* (the composer's term), a dance-like opera in which six characters meet, pass, turn, and return to where they started, with all the classicism and symmetry of a graceful minuet alternating with the free and unexpected moves of a contredanse. The steps and moves are known, yet, in the course of the dance, some element is introduced that makes the dancers pause. Bewildered, and without the usual patterns and codes of behavior in place, they are not sure how to proceed or which way to turn. Some are adventurous and make up new steps as they march forward, while others retire in an effort to return to where they lost their footing. Caught up in the momentum, the dancers follow where the rhythm and the instincts of their natures lead, encircling one another, spiraling, and changing places.

Two of the six players are sisters from Ferrara who are staying (for reasons undisclosed) on their own in a villa by the Bay of Naples, in full sight of the volatile Vesuvius. The year is 1790, just after the French Revolution, and Europe is in a state of vast social upheaval. Yet in this idyllic spot, little disturbs the peace and languor of sun-filled days. The dancers assemble, but their partners have not yet appeared to begin the dance.

The girls, Dorabella and Fiordiligi, are completely in love with their eminently suitable suitors, the handsome military officers Ferrando and Guglielmo. The girls gaze longingly at the images of their fiancés in miniature portraits they wear round their necks. In an almost too-sweet duet, they sing of their lovers' virtues: "This is Adonis/Apollo, more lovely in

Nature than Art, no aspect is wanting in this warrior/lover."
They are young and in love – what could possibly happen to
darken their days?

The dark force who undoes their happiness is Don
Alfonso, an older friend of the two officers who would be the
young men's mentor, guiding them in the ways of the world,
and particularly in the ways of women. Mozart departs
from operatic tradition by opening *Così* with three trios
when the three men meet in a coffee shop. In the first trio,
the officers affirm their faith and trust in the constancy of
their fiancées while Don Alfonso aggravates them by asking,
"Are these two creatures goddesses or are they women, no
more, no less?" He tries to reason with his young friends
on the subject of women's constancy, but his words fall on
deaf ears. The cynical older man has little faith in women
and no time for "blushes, sighs, and palpitations." Is it not
time to take Dorabella and Fiordiligi down from their lofty
pedestals and test the love they proclaim so vehemently? He
good-humoredly proposes a wager of a hundred guineas
that the girls, when tempted, will be unfaithful. Ferrando
and Guglielmo jump at the chance of proving their fiancées'
constancy and winning the bet, and instantly plan to throw
a big party. These are not sophisticated lovers; they, like the
girls, are of the bourgeoisie, and up to this point, life has
been good to all of them.

The test begins when, accompanied by syncopated
strings that describe his pretended agitation, Don Alfonso
tells the girls that their fiancés have been called to war and
must leave at once – this is the first lie. His news leads to a
tearful quintet in which the lovers bid one another tender
farewells as Alfonso chuckles to the audience from the side
of the stage. Martial music summons the men away, and
Alfonso is left with the two girls to sing a hauntingly beautiful

trio, "Soave sa il vento" (O wind gently blowing), in which they pray that the young men will be safe. This exquisite prayer, based on a charade, is the first of many intriguing ambiguities that Mozart and his librettist, Lorenzo Da Ponte, weave into the plot. In *Così* it is far from clear when the characters are serious and when they are parodying themselves, a given situation, or opera itself. Mozart's own position is ambiguous, generously allowing interpretative scope to singers and directors. The music, however, implies that Mozart is firmly on the side of the girls, while the words tell us that Da Ponte, in his pointed libretto, leans towards skepticism.

Da Ponte had personal reasons for his cynical approach to the subject matter for his mistress at the time, a tempestuous soprano called La Ferrarese, was rumored to have been involved in a partner-swapping scandal thus providing the poet with many ideas for the plot. Da Ponte encouraged Mozart to give the role of Fiordiligi to La Ferrarese. While not overly impressed with his friend's mistress, Mozart agreed, and composed the most challenging arias of heroic leaps and falls for her voice.

The mood of farewell which concludes the first scene changes abruptly as Despina, the girls' maid, complains of her lot in life as she samples the hot chocolate she has just prepared for her mistresses. In Despina we meet the opera's sixth and final principal character. The dance partners begin to line up: Dorabella and Ferrando, Fiordiligi and Guglielmo, Don Alfonso and Despina. From here on, the musical and dramatic action concerns itself with the play and interplay of these three pairs in the moves that follow, all within the framework of the duality of the dance, which has brought the dancers face to face. But now the men momentarily leave the floor, supposedly to go to war, and the women dance alone, entwining arms and circling one another.

Bereft and distraught at the departure of their lovers, Despina's mistresses are in no mood for chocolate. Their maid laughs at their distress. She points out that men, especially soldiers, are not expected to be faithful and, should they not return, "There's plenty more to choose from." In a line that 18th-century audiences loved because of its innuendo, Despina assures the sisters "Di pasta simile" (Men are like pasta) suggesting all men are made from the same stuff – pasta! There is a sense of tit for tat happening here: if women are viewed as inconstant and fickle, then maybe men are also, (like pasta), changeable, flexible, even wilting!

When the girls flounce off to their rooms, Don Alfonso takes Despina aside and offers her a gold coin if she will help him introduce two new suitors to the sisters. As cynical as he, Despina agrees at once to be his accomplice, and Alfonso ushers in two young men dressed as Albanian officers. This is the second lie for the two are, of course, Ferrando and Guglielmo. Alfonso uses Despina to test their disguises. Needing her as an ally, he only tells her half the truth. Despina doesn't recognize the "Albanians" and, when the girls enter, she watches delightedly as the two strangers in exotic costumes profess their love for the sisters who are highly insulted and offended at their effrontery. When Don Alfonso arrives a few moments later, he explains that the men are his friends and, like a dance master, begins to direct the girls to new partners.

The individual characters of the four principals, hinted at in the opening scenes, now begin to emerge more clearly. In their first scenes, the sisters express identical sentiments and feelings – they come as a pair, in keeping with the classical symmetry of the plot. But when faced with decisions for which there are no clear guidelines, they react differently. In an astonishing coloratura aria ("Come scoglio immoto resta"), Fiordiligi states that she will stand firm like a rock in the ocean against the advances of any man. This vocal extravaganza borders on parody while challenging the range and pyrotechnics of the best singers. Of the two sisters, Fiordiligi is serious and rational, more likely to follow the rules of reason, though even she admits, at the start of the opera, that she is restless for adventure. The spontaneous Dorabella is more likely to follow the dictates of her heart.

Guglielmo pleads the Albanians' cause in his aria, but the girls continue to insist that the men leave. Once alone, the men congratulate themselves that their fiancées have stood the test of constancy so well, and demand their winnings. "Not so fast," Alfonso says. "It's not over yet." Guglielmo, a good officer, pragmatic and self-assured, does not know how he will suffer later at the collapse of his ideals when Fiordiligi is unfaithful to him. His free-spirited brother-in-arms, Ferrando, sings of love in a meltingly lovely aria, "Un'aura amorosa." But by the end of the opera, Ferrando, too, will discover unanticipated feelings of anger within himself when he learns that his Dorabella is human, "no more, no less," and will say, "The voice of reason is overwhelmed by the conflicting urges of passion!"

In the finale of Act I, the "problems in petticoats," the "unassailable rocks," are under siege. The Albanians stagger into the garden of the villa, where they pretend to drink arsenic in full sight of Dorabella and Fiordiligi before falling to the ground. This ploy catches the girls off guard, but, as women, they have no choice but to rush to the aid of the fallen men. As Dorabella approaches, she admits that "They've a certain strange attraction." In a hilarious scene straight out of commedia dell'arte, Don Alfonso announces the doctor (Despina in disguise), who impersonates Dr. Mesmer – then all the rage in Vienna for his cures with his "mesmerizing" magnet.

Anton Mesmer, the father of hypnotism, believed that an "animal magnetism" drew people together, and that this magnetism accounted for man's social instincts and was the reason and motivation behind human behavior. He also explored spiritual mysticism and the occult, both of which were popular in Europe at the time. Later, his studies and treatments of psychosexual effects eventually discredited him in Vienna. Mozart, poking gentle fun at Mesmer in this funny topical scene, owed much to the doctor, who had presented the young composer's one-act pastorale or *Singspiel, Bastien und Bastienne*, in the garden of his Viennese home many years before, when Mozart was only 12.

As the "doctor," Despina draws a magnet up and down the bodies of the men, removing "negative essences." The Albanians slowly recover and, predictably enough, ask for a kiss from the hovering girls to complete their "cure." The couples, aware now of subtle change, negative essences notwithstanding, are unsure how to proceed as the normal social patterns begin to fall away. The scene ends with a lively sextet: the girls try to stand firm against new and unsettling feelings, the men celebrate the girl's perceived constancy, as Alfonso and Despina comment, "Men desiring, girls refusing, nothing could be more confusing," in the first act's classic Mozartean finale. The dance has speeded up as the four young people approach and withdraw from one another, passing and turning as the curtain falls.

Act II opens with Despina's lecture to her mistresses on how to act as women: "By treating love as a diversion, never miss your chances." Dorabella, beginning to change her mind, suggests to her sister that a mild flirtation could do no harm; "We only seek diversion to ward off melancholy and boredom." Fiordiligi is not so sure, but when Dorabella takes the initiative by deciding to flirt with the dark one (who is not her fiancé), Fiordiligi agrees to "take the fair one, and the comedy begins."

The men arrive in a boat to serenade the girls, and the seduction gets underway in earnest. Choreographed by Alfonso and Despina, the four young people pair up and walk together in different sections of the garden. The flirtation between Dorabella and Guglielmo ends when Guglielmo succeeds in getting Dorabella's locket from her in exchange for a pendant heart he gives her. Dorabella's real heart beats a little faster at the proximity of the attractive Albanian: "I feel like Vesuvius erupting inside," she says as she waltzes off into a shadowed arbor with her new partner.

Fiordiligi, on the other hand, continues to resist the advances of the gallant Ferrando; she is having a difficult time with her conscience. She keeps him at arm's length, though when he leaves, she admits to herself that she is smitten. When the men meet to compare notes, Ferrando is furious to hear Guglielmo boast that Dorabella has succumbed to him; he has not had the same success with Fiordiligi. More firmly resolved than ever to break her resistance, Ferrando returns with impassioned words of love and Fiordiligi also surrenders. The men now find themselves in an unexpected dilemma: they never dreamed the girls would be untrue, but they still love them; jealous, unsure, and out of step, they don't know what to do. Don Alfonso tells them they have nothing to lose; reasoning that if Dorabella and Fiordiligi are untrue, then probably *all* women are untrue, so they may as well marry their erring fiancées, as originally planned. "Così fan tutte" (All women are like that) they sing, it's the way of human nature; the girls must be accepted as they are. The materialistic Alfonso, a man of reason, suggests that human beings generally follow their natural inclinations, and that women are as amenable to being seduced as men are to seduce. Again Mozart, in the words of Don Alfonso, seems to be arguing that men and women are equal, if only in their susceptibility to seduction.

The disgruntled men agree to a double mock wedding, with Despina as the liaison who will provide the notary. An instant wedding is prepared. The Albanians and the women sing together in such a way that it is impossible to tell who is addressing whom – do the men sing to their original loves or to the new ones? In the humor of the moment, and in the music, this could be a ménage à quatre. Despina arrives, disguised as the notary, and the ceremony begins. The girls have just signed the wedding papers when the sound of drums and singing is heard in the distance. The soldiers are returning! Terrified of what will happen, the girls panic. They push the Albanians out of sight and moments later, lo and behold, their own Ferrando and Guglielmo appear in military cloaks. To their horror, the returning officers learn that, in their absence, the girls were about to marry other men. Despina, as the notary, is unmasked. Alfonso tells the men that all the proof they need is in the next room. The men leave, only to return moments later wearing part of their Albanian costumes and singing once again their lines of seduction to the devastated girls.

The dance stalls until Don Alfonso comes forward and admits that the charade was all his doing. His plan was to teach the young people a lesson: "Nothing's perfect here below." He suggests they forgive one another and laugh the matter off, "For there is nothing else to do." The chastened couples take one another's hands as Despina, the know-it-all maid remarks, "Take good care if fooling others; someone else may well fool you."

How the end of the opera should be played is a challenge for 21st-century directors. Earlier generations believed that the only possible outcome was the rational one, in which the girls return to their original lovers. Mozart seems to musically concur: *Così* begins and ends firmly in C major – the circle is complete, the lesson learned, the just order of things reestablished. And yet, in the libretto, Mozart and Da Ponte's intention is not crystal clear – at the end, all four lovers sing together, with no indication as to which suitor is singing to which sister. The traditional ending of *Così* is to return the unraveled dance to its original tempo and rhythm when the players return to their rightful places and partners.

The focus of the opera on the issue of loving two sisters caused Mozart much personal anxiety for he had some first-hand experience of this scenario. Years before he had loved Aloysia Weber, who rejected him, and later fell for her sister Constanze, who accepted him. Like the young men in *Così fan tutte*, Mozart found himself loving one sister and then, some time later, loving her sister equally well. This dilemma troubled the composer for some time. Once married, however, Mozart was true to Constanze, but, well aware that infidelity was a way of life in the 18th century, he was often concerned that her flirtatious behavior would get her into trouble. He wrote to his wife in 1789, when he felt she had been too free with some male acquaintances, "A woman must always make herself respected or else she gets talked about."

When Mozart and Da Ponte address these concerns in this opera of parody and pathos, of lessons and learning, of reason and nature, the voice that raises the questions is that of Don Alfonso. For the director of *Così fan tutte* there are many questions to consider in terms of how Don Alfonso should be played: Is he the wicked perpetrator of the plot, a *philosophe* in the best tradition of the Enlightenment, which suggested that the world was held together by a secular morality of reason, sentiment, and materialism? Or is he a cold investigator interested only, and for his own amusement, in observing the outcome of his social experiment? Is he merely a meddling, vindictive old man who, for whatever reason, is a misogynist? Or is Don Alfonso's a fatherly affection that wants the young couples to understand something of the trials and tests of love and life before taking on the responsibilities of marriage? Is he attempting to put a stop to their posing and blind innocence in order to teach them something of the nature of love? And at what price does all of this come about?

Perhaps we must look to Mozart for a clue to the answers, and to the opera's subtitle: *La scuola degli amanti* (The School for Lovers). Three operas make up this school: *The Marriage of Figaro, Don Giovanni,* and *Così.* In *The Marriage of Figaro,* the overwhelming power of grace and forgiveness following infidelity is the lesson learned; the Countess forgives her erring husband at the end of the opera, and Figaro learns to trust his fiancée, Susanna. The moral stated the end of *The Marriage of Figaro* is "Love can end only in contentment and joy." Don Giovanni's hedonistic lifestyle, in which he destroyed the lives of so many women (1,003 by Leperello's account), results in punishment and damnation. We are told, in the curtain line in *Don Giovanni* that, "Evildoers always come to an equally evil end."

In *Così,* the question of fidelity and constancy comes up yet again. The intricacies of the dance may confuse and amuse but, in the end, the lesson to be learned comes directly from Mozart and the Enlightenment's philosophic toleration of human weakness. The final lines of the opera underscore the lesson in this School for Lovers: "Fortunate is the man who makes the best of everything, and who allows himself to be led by reason."

For some, *Così* describes a fragile, wistful, illusory world whose inhabitants dance carelessly on the crust of a volcano as the world of the ancien régime collapses around them, giving way to a new social order. This story of lost innocence and lost ideals describes not only the loss of romantic love, but the end of an entire way of life

The opera reminds one of a painting by Turner or Watteau in which exquisite young people are seen in misty woodland scenes where Nature herself is depicted as both benevolent and threatening: imagine a young girl sitting in a shaft of warm sunlight in the woods as a storm builds on the horizon behind her. The director of *Così* must decide how to portray this ambivalence and the many ambiguities of Da Ponte's plot and Mozart's music. Comic? Yes. Serious? Yes. Parody and pathos both make up this *dramma giocosa*, which lightly addresses the dance-play between reason, human instinct, and nature.

Characters

Fiordiligi	sisters from Ferrara	soprano
Dorabella	living in Naples	mezzo-soprano
Ferrando, Dorabella's lover		baritone
Guglielmo, Fiordiligi's lover		tenor
Don Alfonso, a philosopher		bass
Despina, a maid		soprano

Bibliography
Brophy, Brigid, *Mozart the Dramatist*, Harcourt, Brace & World Inc., New York, 1964.
Osborne, Charles, *The Complete Operas of Mozart*, Da Capo Press, New York, 1978.
Till, Nicholas, *Mozart and the Enlightenment*, W.W. Norton & Co., New York, 1992.

Intermezzo

Richard Strauss

Ours is what I would call a perfect marriage!
– Christine

*W*hat makes a marriage work? This unfathomable, timeless question is the subject of *Intermezzo*, an opera in which Richard Strauss reveals to the world at large his relationship with his wife, Pauline. He called the opera a "Bourgeois Comedy with Symphonic Interludes," and in it he developed further the musical style he had begun to explore in earlier works such as *Ariadne auf Naxos*. In order to come to grips with this unusual opera, it helps to have a sense of the role Strauss's turbulent marriage played in his work, and where this musical "interlude" fits into his oeuvre overall.

Richard Strauss was the son of Franz Strauss, who for 42 years played horn in the Court Orchestra of Munich; and of Josepha, a member of the great Pschorr dynasty, who are leading Bavarian brewers to this day. Strauss was reared on music and composed from an early age. In 1889, at 25, he took up the post of second Kapellmeister in Weimar and focused on the operas of his idol, Richard Wagner. Good-natured yet occasionally temperamental, Strauss bubbled with enthusiasm in those youthful days, and wrote at length to friends about concerts, operas, performers, Wagner, Brahms, and day-to-day events. As a conductor, he expected the highest standard from his musicians and artists, and had little tolerance for stupidity or insubordination. At the mere suggestion of a cut in his own work or Wagner's, he would fly into an incandescent rage. Loved, hated, respected, admired, Strauss made an impression wherever he went.

Strauss first met the young singer Pauline de Ahna while visiting an aunt in Feldafing, and was immediately attracted to her. He was 23, she 24 and destined to become his wife, his muse, the bane of his life. Pauline's beautiful voice had been trained at the Munich Conservatory, but when she completed her schooling, no professional engagements materialized. Strauss offered to give the attractive if feisty singer voice lessons, and later, with his help, she was contracted to sing at Weimar, where he conducted. Audiences enjoyed her voice, and she had great success singing leading roles in the operas of Mozart and Wagner. When Strauss conducted the premiere of Engelbert Humperdinck's *Hänsel und Gretel* at Weimar in 1893, Pauline sang the role of Hänsel – or nearly sang it, for she broke an ankle running across the stage in rehearsal and had to miss the opening night. In May 1894, Pauline created the role of Freihild in Strauss's first opera, *Guntram*, again achieving a major personal success (though the opera itself did not do well).

One of opera's classic tales is of how, during rehearsals for *Guntram*, Pauline and Strauss got into an argument that ended with Pauline hurling her score at him (she missed, and hit the second violinist's desk instead) and storming off stage to her dressing room, Strauss in hot pursuit. Angry voices were heard, then silence. When the orchestra's leader knocked on the door, Strauss announced that he and Fräulein Ahna were engaged. Later that summer, Strauss conducted *Tannhäuser* at Bayreuth with Pauline singing Elisabeth. As a wedding gift for their marriage in September, Strauss presented his wife with the famous Four Songs, Op. 27. The young composer wrote his most exquisite songs for his wife, and many agreed that no one sang them more beautifully than she when they toured together, Strauss accompanying her on the piano. Pauline then retired to become a housewife, a role she took to neither quietly nor comfortably. As the daughter of a General – a fact she never let Strauss forget – she ruled household and husband with an iron hand

The relationships of famous composers and their wives is one of music's more intriguing aspects. Think of Wagner and Cosima, Mozart and Constanze, Verdi and Strepponi, Puccini and Elvira. Problematical and passionate as these marriages were, none came close to the special histrionics of Richard and Pauline Strauss. Before their marriage, Strauss wrote to her, suggesting that perhaps they should break up, "Since you seem so set on going your way that my presence and influence could only be a burden to you." But after they were married, Strauss defended his wife at every turn. He wrote to his family to ask understanding for Pauline, who, he said, was "unthinking, excited, and over-boisterous, but essentially good-hearted, childlike and naive."

In the early years of their marriage, Pauline often accompanied her husband on tours, sometimes as his soloist, sometimes as his wife. But she didn't like traveling, and eventually chose to stay at home. He, as a famous conductor and composer, traveled extensively, and wrote her long, affectionate letters every day they were apart. When he was at home, Strauss took care of domestic decisions and paid the bills, tasks that fell to Pauline when he was away, much to her annoyance. This state of domestic affairs is graphically described in *Intermezzo*.

The entire musical world gossiped about Pauline – how impossible she was, her latest faux pas, what Strauss had to put up with – one outrageous anecdote followed another. Yet despite her feistiness, or perhaps because of it, theirs was a strong, stable marriage that lasted 55 years. The character of the conductor Storch, who is the voice of Strauss himself in *Intermezzo*, says, "I must have life and temperament around me." It seems that, despite the choppy surface that the outside world saw, the strong undercurrent of affection between husband and wife was sure and constant. Strauss was never unfaithful, and Pauline complemented and suited him well. She saw to it that he got enough rest, the right nourishment, and took daily walks with her. She kept a spotlessly clean house, to the point of fanaticism. Dinner guests were made to wipe their feet before entering their home, then instructed to wash their hands before dinner. Always volatile, highly strung, and very outspoken, Pauline would say the most inappropriate things whenever she felt like it, leaving her resigned husband to mend the fences behind her.

It cannot have been easy for Pauline to give up the spotlight and become merely the wife of a famous composer and conductor. Her ego needed more than that – she needed to be her own person, and was. She provided Strauss with seemingly little support, but he trusted completely this woman who argued with him constantly but who, at some level, also loved him. He was her life. After 36 years of marriage, Strauss, a man who described women with such sensuality in his music, wrote to Pauline that "My inner belonging to you grows greater all the time. I am wholly happy only with you, with our family." Perhaps Strauss summed her up best when he said she was "a sensitive soul who hid herself behind the prickles of a hedgehog." Strauss also loved with an abiding passion the son born of this marriage, Franz – the same little Franz who appears as an eight-year-old in *Intermezzo*.

Much of Strauss's work from this time was modeled on his wife and family. The *Symphonia domestica* of 1902–3, composed after ten years of marriage, is a series of domestic scenes in which Strauss describes mother, father, and baby (Bubi) going for a walk, having supper, preparing for bed, and waking up the next morning. People were shocked and generally critical of Strauss's revelations of the intimacies of his family life in this musical group portrait. Surprisingly, within a year of *Symphonia domestica* Strauss had composed *Salome*, an opera that also shocked, but for very different reasons.

In *Ein Heldenleben* (A Hero's Life), Strauss modeled the Hero's wife on Pauline. "It was my wife I wanted to portray," he said. "She is very complex, very much a woman, a little depraved, something of a flirt, never twice alike. In the beginning the Hero follows her, but she always flies further away. In the end he says, 'I'm staying here' and she comes to him."

When Strauss, composer of so many great tone poems and symphonic music, turned to opera, it became his main focus for the rest of his life. His first major operatic success was in 1905 with the scandalous *Salome*, followed in 1909 by the equally scandalous *Elektra*, called "Elektracution" by one critic for its violence and exploration of atonality. In *Elektra* Strauss collaborated with the man who was to be his partner in his greatest operas, the poet and librettist Hugo von Hofmannsthal. *Der Rosenkavalier*, which followed *Elektra* in 1910, was a deliberate step back by both men from the boundaries of what was possible (or impossible) in music to neo-classicism, and a calmer, gentler mood in the style of Mozart. In *Der Rosenkavalier* the love and tender eroticism that, up to that point, had appeared only in Strauss's songs, now flowered fully in opera.

With *Der Rosenkavalier*, Strauss was firmly established as both a famous composer and a conductor. Then came *Ariadne auf Naxos* – an experiment in a new style of opera in which the first act is almost entirely sung conversation, a technique Strauss was to explore again in *Intermezzo*. *Ariadne* was followed by an opera on the grand scale, *Die Frau ohne Schatten* (The Woman Without a Shadow). In this work, "the bizarre woman with a beautiful soul," Barak's wife, was modeled on Pauline, this time by von Hofmannsthal. This challenging opera required a large orchestra and describes three levels of existence: the spirit world, the world of mankind, and an in-between world. It was composed in the difficult years of World War I and premiered in 1919, a year after war's end. Strauss had kept aloof from politics during the war; he had only two great loves in his life, his wife and family, and his music. He was not to know that he and his family were to endure another world war 20 years later, at great cost.

Intermezzo, the "bourgeois comedy with symphonic interludes," was composed in 1924 in response to Strauss's need for a change of artistic pace following the high drama of *Die Frau ohne Schatten*. He wrote to Hofmannsthal that he wanted to create "an entirely modern, absolutely realistic psychological comedy of character." Hofmannsthal was not interested; "the thing you propose is truly abhorrent to my taste." He suggested that Strauss contact Hermann Bahr, a Viennese dramatist and critic. Bahr asked Strauss to outline the plot he had in mind, the focus of which was an incident that had taken place in Strauss's life some years earlier.

During one of his trips away from home, Pauline had received a note that read, "Dear Herr Strauss, I expected to see you yesterday in the Union Bar, but in vain. I am writing to ask if you will be so kind as to let me have tickets for the opera this week. Yours sincerely, Mieze Mücke." Pauline instantly assumed that her husband was being unfaithful and that she had caught him in the act, so to speak, with this letter. In fury and rage, she wired Strauss at once that she was filing for divorce and putting the matter in the hands of their lawyer.

The totally confused Strauss told his friends about the telegram. It turned out that another conductor, Stransky, whose name was very like Strauss's, had promised Mücke tickets. When Mücke had not heard from the conductor, she looked in the phone book, assumed that Herr Strauss was the one who had promised her the tickets, and mailed the letter. After violent scenes between the Strausses, the matter was sorted out and they were reconciled. This was to be the subject of the new opera.

Strauss was amused by the irony of the incident, in which he, the most perfectly faithful husband, was doubted. In outlining the plot to Bahr, Strauss wrote, in part, "[Storch/ Strauss] loves order. He plans carefully and works hard. She thinks he is a kind of absent-minded professor, remote from the world and always working. That is just her fantasy for she can interrupt his work anytime; he will go for walks and outings with her whenever she wants. When she is excited and busy, she fails to see the purpose of his actions, and this often drives her to despair. Because she feels she is always doing things for him, she longs to be left on her own, but no sooner has he gone away than she experiences great longing for him."

On reading this very personal account, Bahr was uneasy and sure that the sky would fall round his head when Pauline got wind of it. He told Strauss, "You are the only person who can find the right words for this." So Strauss wrote his own libretto, describing his family in dialogue that exactly reproduced what went on in his home. The writing contains the very personalized wit and irony of its composer, who never intended that any of it should be taken seriously. Pauline, on the other hand, saw no humor whatsoever in *Intermezzo*.

Strauss was ingenuous in choosing the opera's title *Intermezzo*, which referred to both operatic short comedies based on contemporary life in the 18th century and to interludes in his own married life.

The opera is in two acts, with eight brief scenes in Act I and five in Act II. Strauss is represented by the conductor Robert Storch, and Pauline by Christine, Storch's wife. The Strauss's young son, Franz, keeps his name, as does their maid, Anna. The action takes place in Vienna and in and around Lake Grundlsee in Austria, by the lake itself, at the ski resort, and in the Storch home. There is no overture; the opera opens to a scene of disorder in the Storch house in which suitcases lie open and clothes are strewn about, waiting to be packed. The mood is one of vexed tension as Christine grumbles at her husband for leaving, complaining of all she has to do while he's away – keep the accounts, answer the phone, choose the menus. Then she starts up an old argument, speaking contemptuously about his inferior family and upbringing, and the fact that he is a mere musician. She orders the servants around, upsetting them and confusing everyone. Finally, to the sound of sleigh bells, Storch leaves as Christine assures him that she will not miss him. She continues to complain after he has gone, as Anna tries to calm her. The phone rings, and Christine agrees to meet a friend to go tobogganing the next day.

This entire lively first scene is musically intriguing for the three kinds of vocal writing heard: sung conversation, half-sung dialogue, and spoken dialogue barely accompanied by the orchestra. A further unspoken conversation is conducted between the voices and the music as the music interprets the words' emotional underpinnings. Strauss sought to retain the naturalness of everyday speech by using a vocal line that followed every inflection of the text. In the Preface to the published score, he described his method of composition. Wanting to pay close attention to natural diction and the pace of dialogue, his aim in *Intermezzo*, he wrote, was to combine speech and recitative, both accompanied and unaccompanied, with melody and *arioso*, all in a single work. He urged conductors to pay special attention to the gradual transitions between the spoken and the sung or half-sung words. The opera is through-composed with no arias, the entire work a fusion of opera and symphonic poem, with no fewer than 12 instrumental interludes

These truly beautiful symphonic interludes provide great richness and depth to the work. The first interlude provides a transition from the scene of vexed farewell to the next day's tobogganing scene. With downward *glissandi* from the violins, one can almost see the toboggans sliding down the snowy hill, one after another. From the top of the hill, Christine cries out "Make way!" and moments later runs her toboggan into a young man on skis. She complains loudly – until she discovers that the young man is Baron

Lummer, the son of a friend of her parents. In the third scene, Christine dances with the Baron as Strauss gives full rein to delicious rustic waltzes. In the fourth, Christine makes arrangements for the Baron to rent a room in the notary's house, giving clear instructions as to how the room is to be kept clean. These brief scenes follow one another quickly, predominated by waltz rhythms that describe Christine and the Baron's lighthearted friendship. Christine is amusing herself, keeping boredom at bay while Storch is away.

The fifth scene is a brief respite from all this lively action as Christine reads a letter she has written to her husband, in which she tells him about her outings with the Baron. Sung and spoken words are interwoven as she reads her letter and comments on it. When the Baron is shown in, she pays him scant attention and busies herself with the newspaper. He tries to ask her a favor, but she doesn't listen, instead singing the praises of her absent husband, "the kindest man in the world, a remarkable man." Finally dismissing the Baron and still missing Storch, she sinks into despondency. The music now comes to the fore in a lovely interlude that approaches a lyric *arioso* as it describes her loneliness with a melodious theme.

A few days later Christine receives a letter from the Baron asking her for a loan of 1000 marks; she realizes she has made a mistake in encouraging the young man. It is while she is speaking to the Baron about his request that the fateful letter addressed to Hofkapellmeister Robert Storch arrives. Christine opens the letter to read "My dear, Let me have two tickets again for the opera tomorrow. Afterwards, in the bar – as usual. Your own Mitzi Mayer." Christine screams with fury, her words confused, scraps of recitative and orchestral interjections describe her anger. She dismisses the Baron abruptly, then telegrams Robert: "I have proof you have betrayed me. We are parted forever." She orders Anna to first send the telegram, then pack their bags.

The act ends with the tearful Christine in Franz's bedroom, telling the child that he will never see his wicked father again. Franz, speaking his lines, defends his father as his mother collapses, sobbing, at his bedside. The orchestra, serious now, describes her pain.

Act II takes us to Vienna, where a group of Robert's friends are playing a game of skat (Strauss's favorite card game) and gossiping about Christine. Stroh, a conductor, takes her side as Robert Storch enters, joins in the game, and launches into a defense of his wife: "I'm so lucky to have as my companion a fiery, fanciful person who, because of her lack of self-control, is often helpless and lost like a child. For me she is the perfect wife, Christine has made me what I am. She is one of those gentle, shy creatures, but rough on the outside."

A maid enters and hands Robert the telegram. He pales. "What is it?" Robert hands the telegram to Stroh. "Read it." At the name Mitzi Mayer, Stroh laughs, "So you know her too?" "I don't know what or whom you are talking about," Robert replies as he leaves the room.

Back home, Christine visits the notary to demand that he start divorce proceedings at once. She is infuriated when the notary assumes it is because of the Baron, whom he knows Christine has been seeing. When he refuses to take the case because of his friendship with her husband, she storms out. The musical interlude that follows this is likewise stormy, expressing first Christine's anger and then, cleverly, as the scene shifts back to Vienna, Robert's anger. He is found pacing back and forth in the rain in the Prater, Vienna's famous park, when Stroh rushes to his side to tell him it was all a mistake – Mitzi's note was meant for him, Stroh. He explains the mixup over the name: by mistake, Mitzi sent her note to Storch instead of to Stroh. Robert is furious and insists that Stroh travel at once to see Christine to explain personally what has happened. The chastened Stroh agrees as the orchestra builds to a frenzied fury.

The orchestra calms down somewhat as it makes the transition to the Storch home, where everything is once more in disarray; Christine is packing. She meets with Stroh offstage, and returns as Robert rushes in to embrace her – but Christine holds him off. They argue, believe it or not, about who was to blame for the whole debacle, and it begins to look as if a divorce really is in the offing after all when, of all people, the Baron enters. Christine quickly sends him away, but not before Robert catches sight of him. "Who is that?" he asks. "The Baron I told you about." Sobered and a little guilty because of her association with the Baron in her husband's absence, Christine tells Robert that the Baron wanted money from her. Robert laughs and teases her: "It is not a good idea that my wife be left alone for too long." With this new development, in which Christine's indiscretion balances Mitzi's letter, the way is cleared for a reconciliation. Husband and wife make up, and, as the curtain falls, Christine categorically states that "Ours is what I'd call the perfect marriage."

As in so many Strauss operas, the musical ending of *Intermezzo* is glorious. With the conflict resolved, Strauss gives full rein to the passion of love and resolution – or, in this case, reconciliation – in an *arioso* style with sweeping vocal lines and soaring melodies from the orchestra.

The casting of Christine in any production of *Intermezzo* is crucial. Strauss chose Lotte Lehmann for this role, an artist whom he highly respected and a personal family friend. Lehmann had lived for some weeks with the Strauss family in Garmisch while Strauss coached her for *Die Frau ohne Schatten*. The singer said of this time: "These were interesting and wonderful days. We studied much and in between I took air baths with the very earthy Pauline Strauss. She is such a character [*Sie ist so originell*]." The three were close friends. In the evenings, Lehmann would sing lieder to Strauss's accompaniment. Pauline, a fresh-air fiend, insisted Lehmann do strenuous calisthenics with her every day on the floor. Lotte understood more than most that the Strauss marriage was a truly happy one, despite appearances. Of the composer, she wrote, "One was simply not [Richard's] friend: he drew a wall about himself and his family – his works were the children of his spirit." Lehmann's challenge in *Intermezzo* was to portray Christine-Pauline sympathetically. She said, "Investing the role of Christine with a measure of charm proved to be a difficult task." She must have succeeded; critics said of her performance, "In the role of the temperamental, passionate wife Lotte Lehmann offered an unsurpassable achievement of rare truthfulness and naturalness, with a thoroughly sympathetic undertone."

The Strauss family insists that Pauline did not know, when she took her seat in the Staatsoper in Dresden in November 1924, that she was the subject of *Intermezzo*. The row about it began when she and Strauss returned to their hotel that night, and raged on for two days. But, like the opera, it ended in reconciliation – as all their rows ended over the many years they were together.

Strauss composed seven more operas after *Intermezzo*. His final work, *Capriccio*, was composed in 1940–1, during the tumultuous and difficult years of World War II, Hitler, and the Nazis. Another conversational piece, *Capriccio* focused on the discussion about which is more important in opera, the words or the music.

The period following the end of World War II was a time of extreme privation for the Strauss family, who struggled in their home in Garmisch to make ends meet. The day after the destruction of the Vienna Staatsoper, Strauss composed *Metamorphosen*, a study for 23 solos strings. The exquisite *Four Last Songs* were composed in 1948.

Strauss and Pauline were allowed to leave for Switzerland shortly after the end of the war, but ultimately they returned home to Garmisch in 1949, just before his 85th birthday. Strauss was disillusioned, his health poor, and he was deeply saddened by the destruction of the great opera houses in which he had worked his entire life. He died later that year. Pauline, who was beside her husband every day of the war-torn years, survived her beloved Richard by eight months. They are buried side by side in Garmisch.

Characters

Christine Storch	soprano
Hofkapellmeister Robert Storch, her husband	baritone
Franz, their son	speaking part
Anna, their maid	soprano
Baron Lummer	tenor
The Notary	baritone
His wife	soprano
Stroh, the conductor	tenor

Bibliography

Glass, Beaumont, *Lotte Lehmann: A Life in Opera and Song*, Capra Press, California, 1988.
Osborne, Charles, *The Complete Operas of Richard Strauss*, Da Capo Press, New York, 1988.
Sadie, Stanley, ed., *The Grove Dictionary of Opera*, Macmillan Reference Ltd., London, 1998.
Wilhelm, Kurt, *Richard Strauss: An Intimate Portrait*, Thames & Hudson, London, 1989.